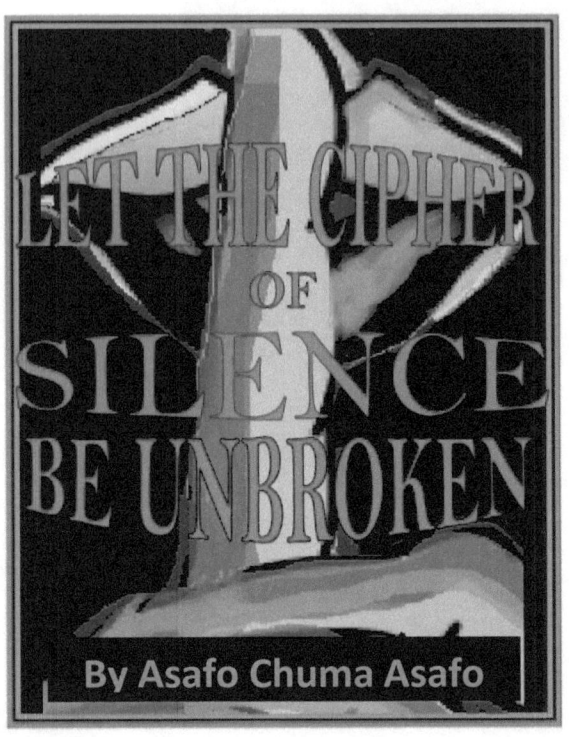

LET THE CIPHER OF SILENCE BE UNBROKEN

By Asafo Chuma Asafo

PRINTED AND PUBLISHED BY: LEGATEE INK PUBLISHING

1623 Dalton Street #14939

Cincinnati, Ohio 45250

Layout & Illustrations

Queen Tahiyrah Asafo

© LEGATTE INK PUBLISHING 2017

" ... Given the power dynamics between Blacks and whites, with whites being the ones in power - it is only to the detriment and disadvantage of Blacks (as a whole) when they run to the white man to snitch or otherwise betray their own. Quite frankly, it is downright despicable."

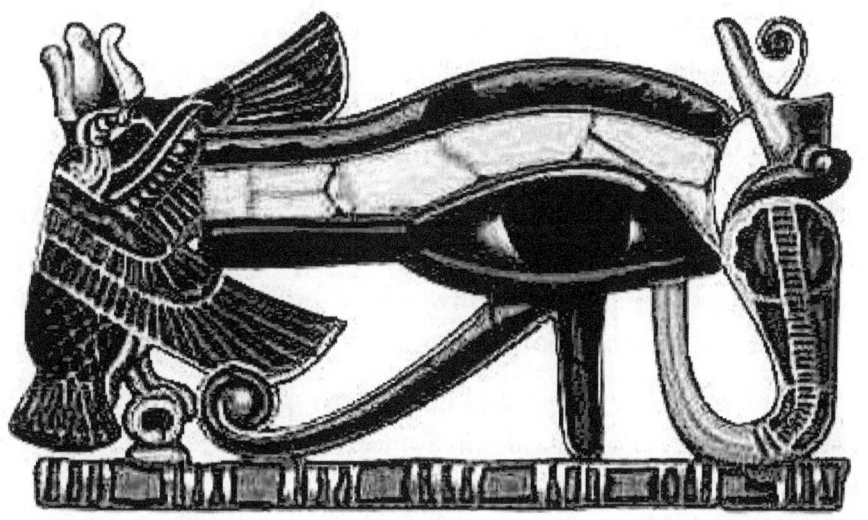

- IRON EYE

ANATOMY OF A SNITCH:

A WARNING TO THE STREETS

IT IS NO SECRET that a snitch is, uniformly, one of the most abhorred and hated people among any circle - whether it be in the business world, an exclusive club, a political party, a religious organization, a street-fraternity (so-called gang), or in the everyday social setting.

In recent years, the snitch phenomenon has reached epidemic proportions and has gone virtually unabated, leaving the Black community in ruins. So herein we will attempt to shed some light on this putrid phenomenon and its constituent elements.

Webster's dictionary describes a snitch thusly: An Informant; To Turn Informer; To Squeal on Someone. A snitch is known by many other relative titles: Stoolpigeon, Fink, Rat, Turncoat, Traitor, et al. However, no matter the title the ultimate end is betrayal. And, according to an old Street maxim, "Betrayal is the bastard son of cowardice".

The most common known quisling is the so-called LAW-ABIDING CITIZEN, who routinely co-operates with the "Established Authority" out of a conditioned, albeit misplaced, sense of duty; and (genuinely) feel in his heart that he's doing the

"Right Thing". The Law-Abiding Citizen views anyone not in compliance with the laws set up and enforced by the 'Established Authority", as a CRIMINAL. Of course, his definition of CRIMINAL, much like his views in general, is manufactured and readily provided to him by the Established Authority which, in this instance, is the Amerikkkan government and its myriad law-enforcement agencies. The so-called LAW-ABIDING CITIZEN (in this context) is a modern helot (mentally), and functions, in most cases, as an unwitting servant of the oppressive Amerikkkan system. And because of his (Induced) state of historical amnesia, he has forgotten that the government and its repressive laws, which he so obediently adheres to, are founded on the kidnap, rape, murder and enslavement of Afrikan people; not to mention the mass slaughter of the Natives (so-called Indians) and the ILLEGAL seizure of their (this) land, thereby rendering the Amerikkkan government the archetype or original criminal, which in turn gave birth to the so called Law-Abiding Citizen. So, those who comply with or abide by the very laws fashioned and perpetuated by the Original Criminal literally becomes agents of the original criminal, thus (proxy) criminals themselves.

And since whites (in general) are the primary beneficiaries of said laws, they are serving their overall interests when they cooperate with the Established Authority. Conversely, when Blacks and other non-whites co-operate with the repressive government, in the vein of being a Law-Abiding Citizen, especially at the peril or detriment of their own endemic ethnic or racial group, respectively, makes them traitors!

Such treachery determined the fate of one of the Black Liberation Movement's most beloved and promising leaders: Comrade Fred Hampton, who was brutally gunned down by the FBI and Chicago police, after being provided blueprint schematics of his "Safe House" and other vital information, by a snitch, a traitor

4

named William O'Neal, who felt he was doing the "Right Thing" - To which NBLA Chairman Knab A. Asafo once quipped:

"The best remedy for a traitor is a bullet."

In fact, several Black Liberation Warriors were either assassinated or imprisoned with the collaborative efforts of snitches. In some cases, were strategically infiltrated into Black Liberation formations, viz: The Black Panther Party, The Black Guerrilla Family Liberation Army, The Nation of Islam, The 5 Nation of Gods & Earths among others. Some were moles who sat and grew within these formations and reported their plans and activities to the Established Authorities.

Others were AGENTS PROVOCATEURS, whose sole purpose was to initiate and agitate dissension, and to cause disorder in the ranks. Also, to provoke "trouble" - to effect expose said organizations to being CRIMINALIZED, to justify the government's aggressions against them.

----- THE OPPORTUNIST SNITCH -----

The opportunist snitch is one who is completely devoid of loyalty. He is prone to betray anything or anyone to aggrandize himself. Such a snitch is neither here nor there, in terms of commitment. He acts, inherently, as a double agent; a chameleon, who blends in with his environment or respective group, for PERSONAL favor. Much like the proverbial YARD-SLAVE in the days of chattel slavery.

On slave plantations, the slaves (and the enslaved) were recognized in three distinct categories: THE FIELD-SLAVE, THE HOUSE-SLAVE and the seldom talked about YARD-SLAVE. There was a clear-cut distinction between the field-slaves and the house-slaves, But the yard-slave was a bit more difficult to figure out, because-of his many levels of craftiness and feigned loyalty. For instance, in his bid to gain favor with the slave master he would often snitch on the field-slaves' plans to escape; planned rebellions, etc. Likewise, the yard-slave would provide the field-slaves with information concerning the slave master's activities. Of course, the yard-slave was very surreptitious in his handling of both parties.

He would often receive frivolous trinkets for snitching: A piece of (fried) chicken and maybe a (buttered) biscuit. The YARD-SLAVE was dubbed such because he functioned both characteristically and literally between the HOUSE and the FIELD. However, today he is aptly known as the OPPORTUNIST SNITCH. Sure, the times have changed but the motives and characteristics are still the same.

The opportunist snitch of today is one who would run to the police to settle his business (in the streets) rather than handle it himself. Even the so-called street-level gangster. If observed closely, the so-called street-level gangster who displays a

6

conspicuous love and reverence for his material possessions, i.e., Cars, Clothes, Jewels, etc., above his loyalty and commitment to his friends, family & comrades, is likely to betray his friends, family & comrades in favor of said material possessions; even SNITCH if necessary.

And, since most people (in this hyper-capitalist class society) openly worship materialism, they often make the (fatal) mistake of deeming someone COOL or THOROUGH, not by their characters, their principles, or their merits of loyalty - but by the clothes they wear, the car they drive, and a host of other abextra facades.

The opportunist is utterly self-centered. He is motivated by wanton narcissism, He doesn't regard any group or social interests above his own. He will betray anyone to those who can best serve his (personal) interests. Historically speaking, it was the OPPORTUNIST SNITCH who squealed on Warrior Ancestor Gabriel Prosser; A Bold Black Freedom Fighter, who was

Gabriel Prosser

planning a massive Slave revolt on plantations throughout the entire state of Virginia, back in the early 1800's. But it was halted before it could be fully carried out. The slave master was tipped off, and Gabriel was charged with Sedition, (mock) tried, convicted and immediately hanged.

His only crime was his desire to strike a mighty blow at the wretched slave system. And for this, he was betrayed by the opportunist snitch. Nonetheless, some thirty years later he gained redemption incarnated in warrior ancestor Nat Turner, who led a relatively successful revolt in South Hampton Virginia. It should be noted; Nat Turner was very meticulous in weeding out and avoiding snitches. Undoubtedly, a lesson learned from his courageous predecessor.

A more popular scenario is the story of Judas Iscariot, who was one of Jesus' most trusted disciples - who ratted on Jesus to the Centurion (Roman police) for thirty pieces of silver. An ancient paragon of the OPPORTUNIST SNITCH.

Judas Iscariot

In this day & time, and in this dog-eat-dog society (Amerikkka), the opportunist snitch is given more & more opportunity to snitch, with lesser & lesser repercussion or punishment. It is often iterated that we are living in the INFORMATION AGE, where informants are in high demand; and, where information can either make you or break you (depending on who has it and how it is used).

The proliferation of snitching is a direct reflection of this information boom (and the demand for it); especially since information, for the most part, is controlled by the government and its many agencies (for its benefit). Hence, the government breeds informants, whether with financial incentives, deception, torture, or as a form of negotiation, especially in getting out of so-called ILLEGAL situations where there are multiple so-called perpetrators (in an alleged crime). In such situations lies are always used to bolster the state's justifications to criminalize, prosecute and ultimately do away with its intended target.

The lack of punishments being handed down to snitches is even reflected in the government's protection of them, as it has grown ostensibly lax. There used to be a strict policy of confidentiality provided for snitches who cooperated with the government - hence CONFIDENTIAL INFORMANT - and the WITNESS PROTECTION PROGRAM. However, in recent years, these protections have become noticeably obsolete, with the lack of repercussions being meted out to snitches.

An example of this can be gleaned from the pages of recent Mafia history, with infamous snitch, Sammy "The Bull" Gravano being a salient figure for snitching on famous mob boss John Gotti. Sammy was excused of thirteen (admitted) murders in

Artist rendering of the trial.

exchange for his testimony. And he eventually returned to the streets (unprotected).

He was even arrested again for running a multi-million-dollar drug ring. He apparently has no fear of reprisal. And the fact that he is still alive, despite said lack of protection, is a testament to the times in which we live. In fact, he has even opened the floodgates for a throng of other "Wise Guy" types, who opt to cooperate with the government as a way of simply doing business. In this context, the once sacred code of OMERTA (code of Silence) is a relic, and only exists as mere folklore in the annals of "Mafia" history.

Another example can be discerned from the brief history of Philadelphia's Junior Black Mafia (JBM), and its infamous snitch Rodney "Frog" Carson, who ratted on his crew. And just like Sammy The Bull, he remains in the hood (unprotected). The fact that he is still alive is blasphemy to the "Code of The Streets" and its(professed) adherents.

In a more broader scope, snitching has become an accepted social reality - an open secret. Mainstream (corporate owned) media, e.g. PRINT, RADIO BROADCAST, TELEVISION, INTERNET, etc., openly solicits and encourages snitching, especially as it pertains to the powerless and the oppressed; for them to place an honorable mask on an otherwise shameful face of dishonor.

Moreover, to associate with a known snitch is to share a tacit complicity of sorts. Because to fail to cogently condemn it (in whatever way the situation calls for) is a form of acceptance. At the very least, the known snitch should be exposed to others who may not be aware of him.

In the mid-1800s, at the height of the famous UNDERGROUND RAILROAD escape led by warrior ancestor Harriet Tubman (and others), there arose many OPPORTUNIST SNITCHES who attempted to seize upon the opportunity to gain favor with the slave master by divulging the identities of the Underground Railroad leaders and their escape routes. However, such snitches were swiftly punished or (in most cases) put to death. Such measures were not out of malice, but rather as a necessity, to protect all parties involved, and to maintain an absolute secrecy on the railroad to freedom. For, failure to do so would have indubitably resulted in the death of all involved. Again, a snitch is a detriment to any respectable group or formation, and should be shunned, condemned, and in most cases, returned to the essence.

--- THE MAKING OF A SNITCH ---

It is often (rhetorically) uttered that a Person who snitches 'Has Snitch in Their Blood', is "A Born Snitch" etc. Such prattle is hollow, and is rooted in thin air. The reality is, much like other characteristics that manifest themselves in the behavioral patterns of a people (especially a subjugated people), it is created by the dominating group, transmuted through externally influenced conditions, and incubated within the circumference of the controlled vicissitudes of a pre-fabricated milieu. Simply put, an informant is the by-product of his environment; which then begs the question of - Who is it that creates and controls the conditions of said environment? The answer is an obvious one, as it is no big secret that the white owned & operated Amerikkkan Government openly wields manipulative power and influence (with the ever-present threat of force) over the society at large, and clearly prolong its position of power through the use of collaborators, political conformists, informants and the like.

Nonetheless, even under an oligarchical, racist white power structure such as this one (Amerikkka), there exists what is commonly referred to as a SUB-CULTURE. And this so-called sub- culture encompasses the many respective ethnic communities that comprises the Amerikkkan society, e.g., CHINA-TOWN, LITTLE ODESSA, LITTLE HAVANA, LITTLE ITALY, THE BLACK COLONY (THE HOOD/GHETTO), among others. And within these respective so-called sub-cultural, ethnic groups, exists a core code of conduct that traditionally condemns snitching. This was especially so within the Black colony (once upon a time). The same for other social taboos that occasionally infiltrated the culture via, but not limited to, the forms of media mentioned earlier.

But judging from the exponential growth and rapidity of snitching among Blacks nowadays, we have obviously abandoned our old traditions, thereby allowing the snitch mentality to fester and permeate the culture. The conscious Elders of the community have been silent and inactive in their condemnation of this shameful behavior, thus leaving the culture vulnerable to the repressive white governmental structure, to be fashioned into a snitch sub-culture - in service of the white rulers.

On a more mundane level, a snitch can be created or made especially in a so-called common criminal predicament - by coercion, trickery, fear, or plain 01' psychological manipulation. For instance, recently while reading a Philadelphia Daily Newspaper, I came across a very interesting story about a young Black couple who were being charged (as co-defendants) in a drug case.

The paper went on to say that the young woman (defendant) was removed from her jail cell (in the middle of the night) and taken to a local FBI field office. The paper further stated that: "It is purported that she is seeking to cut a deal. It was, however, later uncovered that the FBI were in fact the ones who surreptitiously "LEAKED" this bogus story to the paper. However, with the story not being confirmed as true (as journalism goes) the paper cleverly used the term 'PURPORTED" to maintain a thin veil of journalistic integrity, while at the same time protecting themselves from civil liability, and to camouflage their deceptive intent, which was to play upon the oversight of the casual reader. Take notice how the word PURPORTED looks and sounds like REPORTED. But they differ in meaning. Purported means RUMORED.

And since people (in general) tend to believe everything they read in the newspaper (on face value), the feds knew it would place her in the spotlight of suspicion among her peers, especially her co-defendant. The tactic worked. Once she was released on bail, she was met with death threats, and generally shunned by her peers. She was then contacted by the (FBI) agent assigned to her case, who expressed, in no uncertain terms, that she might as well co-operate now, since everybody already thinks she's a rat. She eventually succumbed and became the government's star witness (against her co-defendant). She felt like she was put in a DAMNED-IF-I-DO, DAMNED-IF-I- DON'T situation which, without her knowledge, was initiated and precipitated by the government.

The Amerikkkan government has a sordid history of manipulating information and situations to place targeted individuals (or groups) in the shadow of ill-repute among their respective peers, organizations, etc. Such BROWN-MAIL tactics were employed against one of the Black Power Movement's most charismatic spokesmen, Comrade Kwame Ture (formerly Stokely Carmichael). The government's secret police or Counter

Kwame Ture
(formerly Stokely Carmichael)

Intelligence Program (COINTELPRO) headed by then FBI director J. Edgar Hoover, spread a vicious rumor among the Pan-Afrikan-Revolutionary community that comrade Kwame Ture was an informant. This was done to isolate him from the broader elements of the movement. However, rather than shrink from or succumb to such spurious detractions, he openly called the government out on it, to prove it. Needless to say, they couldn't; as a lie always falls apart in the presence of truth.

Kwame's reputation was promptly restored, and he continued to struggle on behalf of Afrikans here in the hells of Amerikkka and

in the broader diaspora, until he was eventually felled by cancer, which was purported to be the CIA's weapon of choice, to assassinate him.

"It is the inherent duty of all (FBI) agents to convert targeted subjects into informants; especially blacks and other minorities."

- TYRONE POWERS (EX-FBI AGENT)

Another more familiar tactic which, believe it or not, is still used today, with unbelievable success, is the "Prisoner's Dilemma"

method which entails the separating of two (or more) so-called co-conspirators and leading the other(s), through lies & deceit, to believe that the other(s) are willing to co-operate, thereby eliciting a definitive statement from (at least one) against the other(s). Thus, THE MAKING OF A SNITCH. This form of ratting is generally known today as: "GETTING DOWN FIRST."

"Can't be too safe 'cause niggas Is two-faced, they show the other side when they catch a new case."
JAY-Z

----- THE LOOSE-LIPS SNITCH -----

THE LOOSE-LIPS SNITCH is more so stupid, albeit negligent, than malicious. He is usually un-cultured, and quite fond of prattling. A secret is inconsequential to him. His reckless babbling often results in trouble for people (other than himself). He simply doesn't know what to say, how to say it, why to say it, when to say it, where to say it, nor whom to say it to.

The loose-lips snitch is usually of insignificant stature, in terms of his status (within his respective peer group); so he takes great (personal) pleasure in openly discussing other peoples' business (in public). His pseudo sense of importance is measured by him being privy to, in most cases, distorted pieces of information deemed arcane relative to his insignificant livelihood. He is the number one purveyor of rumors.

Moreover, he doesn't see himself as a snitch; which essentially renders him that much more dangerous. His unscrupulous insensitivity to secrecy makes him, unwittingly, a carrier of (often false) information, at the behest of his unbridled tongue. He can easily become an agent, unbeknownst to his own self. He gives full meaning to the age-old adage: "LOOSE LIPS SINKS SHIPS."

---THE DRY SNITCH ---

The person who Dry Snitches does so in such a sly and indirect manner, to absolve themselves of the guilt of doing it flat-out; as we" as to maintain an outward appearance of being a stand-up individual. He is we" aware that snitching is wrong and shameful. This is why such tacit methods are employed. He bears striking similitude to the OPPORTUNIST SNITCH in that his motives are self-centered, but functions more so from an uncontrollable, emotional impulse.

Recently, I saw a situation on the (real-life) TV program COPS, where two young Black men were pulled over by the police for what appeared to be DWB (Driving While Black). At any rate, they were both ordered from the vehicle, at which time One of the (white) cops began searching the two men while the other searched the car. The one searching the car found a handgun. Both men were immediately handcuffed. The cop then asked one of the young men: "Who does this firearm belong to?" And the young man replied: "It's his car, ask him", referring to the other young man. Apparently, he didn't want to flat-out snitch, but he was also afraid of being arrested. Therefore, he uttered: "It's his car ... " so as to imply that the gun must be his as well. So, although dry, he snitched nonetheless. After all, he did have the option to just remain SILENT!

"You have the right to remain silent."

- 5th AMENDMENT

--- THE JAIL-HOUSE SNITCH ---

JadaKiss

"Why is rattin' at an all-time high, why are they even alive? - JADAKISS

The jail-house snitch is a combination of the OPPORTUNIST SNITCH, the LOOSE-LIPS SNITCH and the DRY SNITCH. He is the ultimate STOOLPIGEON.

Because prisons are inherently condensed, microcosmic, sub- societies, it is virtually impossible for a snitch to maintain complete anonymity. Unlike the more macrocosmic or larger society, paranoia and suspicion is on a perpetual high; mainly because of the compelled co-existence in a multi-ethnic, artificial environment.

So the slightest fraternization between prisoner & captor (prison official) can easily be construed as a fundamental form of capitulation (on the part of the prisoner), and can result in said prisoner being excommunicated from his respective ethnic or general social group.

However, once a prisoner is definitively identified as a snitch he's usually dealt with in a more corporal manner (depending on the circumstances and the prison).

In a clinical context, the prisoner who openly befriends his captor can be classified under the STOCKHOLM SYNDROME, which is defined as a developed emotional attachment to a captor formed by a prisoner because of stress, protracted dependence and a (misplaced) need to cooperate for survival. However, if this Stockholm Syndrome isn't counterbalanced with the real threat of punishment or death it will eventually contaminate the whole population (in one form or another). It is a virtual cancer that, in this context, if not cut out immediately, will threaten the entire body (politic) of the denizens of said condensed environment.

And because prisons (in Amerikkka) are almost completely staffed & run by racist whites, who view their occupation as the perfect opportunity to unmask their innate hatred, and to perpetrate their petty, personal agenda against Black and other non-white prisoners who, by the way, make up a large demographic of the Prison Industrial Complex - any prisoners - especially Blacks or other non- whites, found cooperating with said racist captors, is doubly detested (and rightfully so), as it represents the ultimate act of betrayal, in favor of the repression of the already oppressed!

And, the few black officials who work on these modern-day slave ships (on dry land) are often seven-times worse than their (white) Colleagues. They are the neo-overseers for their modern white slave masters.

Traditionally, within the prison environment snitches were almost always segregated in a special Protective Custody Unit, for fear of being either beaten or killed. However, nowadays snitches are more fluent in the general populations, where they serve as human surveillance cameras for prison authorities. They are even used as witnesses, where they are often (strategically) placed in the same cell or general living quarters of pre-trial defendants, to gather information concerning pending cases, at the behest of the government, in exchange for leniency in their own legal situations (or some other favors).

"A fool's mouth is his destruction, and his lips are the snare of his soul,"

- PROVERBS, 18:7

--- RESOLUTION ---

Amerikkka's jails and prisons are filled with scores of good Brothers & Sisters, many serving lengthy sentences (some on Death Row) because of the lies and fabrications of snitches & turncoats. And this will continue to determine the fate of the Black colony if so-called "THOROUGH" or "CONSCIOUS" individuals just stand by, doing nothing. Or, even worse, if snitches are made to feel comfortable and accepted by Thorough or Conscious individuals. There should always be penalties for snitches.

Therefore, in an effort to reverse the vicious cycle of snitching, the young have to be taught against it, and shown (by example) the virtues of loyalty. After all, what could be said of the elders of a particular group - whether it be racial, ethnic, fraternal or what have you - that allows its young to grow up without proper instruction? If the elders neglect their duty in this regard, it will eventually come back to haunt them, in the long run (and rightfully so)!

So, what we propose is that all known snitches be ostracized and exiled from the hood. And if they are caught in the hood they should be penalized by the warrior-class of the hood. Pictures (or snipe- style posters) of known snitches should be posted throughout the hood. This also goes for pedophiles (child molesters), child killers, and those who prey on the elderly and the disabled. If those who perform these acts are caught in the hood they should be punished by the hood.

The racist police establishment should never come into the equation.

Web sites should be formed (guerilla-style) to apprise the concerned public of the identities of rats; revealing their entire profiles, whereabouts, etc (www.snitch.com)??? Their entire dossiers are of public record once they squeal to the "ESTABLISHED AUTHORITY". There should be nowhere for them to hide. A snitch should never be able to do it twice. Also, and more important, there should be more fear of the hood (for a snitch) than that of the racist police establishment!

DEATH TO THE SNITCH!!!

--- THE SNITCH FACTOR: ---
GROUND ZERO

"In a culture where Individualism and self- centered tendencies takes precedence over altruistic principles, it should come as no surprise then that today's snitch culture Is just as prevalent: For snitching denotes the ultimate act of selfishness. And Its widespread acceptance these days, as oppose to that of a bygone era, is the manifestation of its streamlined effect upon the society (as a whole)."

-- IRON EYE

While the above stated is a synopsis of today's snitch rate, its increasing fluency and open acceptance, (in the now times), versus that of a 'bygone era', it indicates something much deeper, as snitching, when examined more viscerally, highlights Black peoples' powerlessness within the context of their sub-integrationist, existence in this white dominated society (Amerikkka).

> Never discuss cheese with rats, talk bread with birds or make moves with snakes...

Interestingly, in a haste to promote the ABSOLUTE or CUT & DRY posture of the "STOP SNITCHING" decree that is preached within the hood, we tend to overlook some pertinent factors that, conversely, contribute to its proliferation. At the very crux of this social defect is the iniquitous power dynamics between the two racial groups, with whites being the undisputed power holders over the very existence of Black and other non-white peoples. And in this vein, the entire gamut of nuances regarding the practice of snitching needs to be more closely examined in order for us to fully & honestly get to the bottom of, and, perhaps curtail this treasonous behavior.

On the one hand, there's the plain old fear of whites (and their power to alter the lives of the powerless at their whim), along with outright cowardice, which is, in part, a cross between said fear factor and a general lack of cultural refinement or consciousness (on the part of Black people) which is essentially rooted in the slave system that is the very foundation of this society. On the other hand, since snitching (historically) was regarded by Black people (in particular) as siding with the white man, who was generally understood to be the enemy, it wasn't as rampant (back in the day) as it is today.

So, this logically raises the question of: What Has Changed? Well, among the myriad elements that can be cited, undoubtedly, the advent of the crack-cocaine plague that swept through the Black colony like a wildfire, obliterating the moral parameters of both the user and the dealer, subsequently giving rise to the mindless gang culture that has become so prevalent in the hood has to be the most telling.

And, unlike other ethnic or racial groups, who have (historically) formed secret-societies or even street-fraternities (so-called gangs) to empower and protect their respective groups, the young black so- called-street thug, being, first of all, devoid of culture and therefore his loyalty and obligation to his people (community/nation), has put his community in a catch-22 where, in one sense, the community is naturally reluctant to go to the police, as the police establishment represents the racist and brutal continuity of the slave system - with its present-day and ever expanding Prison Industrial Complex being nothing short of a modern revision of historical slave plantations.

In another sense, the very people who should be providing empowerment and protection for the Black community are the very people terrorizing it with Black-or-Black gang warfare running amok in the hood, and women, children and the elderly increasingly becoming (incidental) casualties in the quasi turf wars that have become commonplace; forcing the community to call on our collective enemy (the repressive police establishment) for help.

"Back In the days our parents used to take care of us/ look at 'em now, they're even fuckin' scared of us/ callin' the city for help 'cause they can't maintain/ damn, shit done changed."

-NOTORIOUS B.I.G.

--- BETRAYAL BEGETS BETRAYAL ---

Hypocritically, the constituents of this mindless Black-on-Black destruction urges the very communities they're destroying to keep their mouths shut, or to "STOP SNITCHING". That is to say, they wish to go (uninterrupted) in their abnegating quest to destroy and terrorize the women, children and elders of their own communities. Apparently, it hasn't occurred to them that they simply cannot have it both ways. Snitching, without question, is an act of betrayal. But is not the neglect or failure to protect one's own, equally so?

The very essence of humanity is premised on security and protection from harm, etc. So, when this cannot be found within the family = community = nation, it will naturally be sought elsewhere. Whenever the women, children and elders of a racial or ethnic group calls upon another ethnic or racial group (especially their white oppressors) to save them from the young men of their own endemic group, it delineates the powerlessness of the entire group. And it is shameful.

Back in the day, if someone raped, killed or otherwise harmed a child or an elder in the hood, his corpse would be found in a vacant lot (or not found at all). And if the police got to him before the hood got him, he would not survive in any prison population, because he would be killed. In those days, the MEN of the Black colony assumed the power (in and of themselves) to exact punishments upon those who violated those who were "off limits", i.e., Women, Children and Elders.

In situations of minor disputes where talking wouldn't suffice, fist fights were in order. And if weapons came into the play, certainly no children or innocent bystanders were felled or injured. However, when the spirit of Black liberation began to take hold within the Black colony, it articulated and contextualized the powerlessness and the axis of oppression as being the direct result of the machinations of the white "powers that be."

In the struggle to gain power and to wrest free of the white man's pernicious domination, the Code of Silence became more deliberate & purposeful. This represented GROUND ZERO, as Black self-determination, Black self-definition and Black self- rulership was/is somehow construed as a "crime" in the minds of the white supremacist ruling elite. The New-Afrikan principle of KIMYA (silence) was strictly enforced. And as the Black Liberation movement gained momentum, it became generally understood that any quisling (by anyone) would be dealt with accordingly. For, in the reconstruction of a People's self-governance (or nation-building) it is necessary to weed out the loose-lips "negroes". In fact:

"Every Nationalist Revolutionary formation throughout history, has taken up the task of neutralizing its informants and traitors, to safeguard the revolution."

--- IRON EYE

And the more culturally (and politically) conscious the Black colony became the more empowered they felt, which in turn illustrated their potential for real, tangible independence. And since the very foundation of white domination is ostensibly predicated on Black people's powerlessness, any real movement toward Black Power had to be effectively rolled Back by the repressive Amerikkkan government. And this required a vast network of informants and other traitors; those who were willing to betray the burgeoning revolution. And considering this stepped-up counter-intelligence agenda by the federal government, warrior Messenger Elijah Muhammad admonished that:

"They tap our telephones, eavesdrop and follow us around from place to place, and use recording devices; and the hypocrites and stoolpigeons among us keep them up to date on what we say and do. They are bold enough to even ask your own relatives to help them to do you evil; and due to fear and Ignorance on the part of my poor people, the enemy hires them to destroy themselves."

In reality, nobody likes a snitch. The oppressor, who always finds use for them (to protect and prolong his rulership) doesn't like nor respect them. He reasons that, if they will squeal on or otherwise betray their own, then they are the lowest of the low; therefore, the oppressor doesn't trust them beyond their (treasonous) use.

Interestingly, when whites squeal, it is commonly referred to euphemistically, as "Whistle Blowing". Inner-race snitching, with White folks informing on themselves (or on- others), or even Blacks telling on whites (to other whites of course), in contrast to Blacks snitching on other Blacks (to whites) carries very different ramifications. Blacks being the powerless party, are in no position to either (systematically) determine or alter the fate of whites. So, any whites found collaborating with Blacks (on Blacks' terms) are merely deemed nigger-lovers". Conversely, any Blacks found collaborating with whites (on their terms) are traitors! For, the power disparities between the two is the ultimate determining factor, as the powerful doesn't see eye to eye with the powerless. The powerful holds the power to arbitrarily determine the fate of the powerless (as they see fit). Therefore, any co-operation/collaboration with the oppressor's inherently racist police apparatus represents both, an acquiescence and a coalescence with the oppressor; an open agreement with their rulership over (and the police-state style occupation of) the Black colony.

It is within this unholy arrangement (of contradictory sorts) where we see the Black community, on the one hand, call for an end to the (Black-on-Black) violence that's wreaking havoc on the hood. While on the other, the Black community urges the hood to ignore the "STOP SNITCHING" campaign and to "KEEP TALKING" (to the enemy of us all). This, likewise, puts the young Black so called street thug in a catch-22.

The contradiction is that, in one vein, he is encouraged to respect and protect his community, while at the same time being turned in to the police establishment by the very community he's expected to protect & respect. This contradiction is exacerbated even further, given the fact that the repressive police apparatus doesn't even respect the Black

Abner Louima & Atty. Johnny Cochran

community itself. For its flagrant brutality and reckless disregard for the denizens of the hood is well documented - as images of the

Rodney King beating still looms large in the (collective) consciousness of Blacks in this racist country; including the savage Abner Louima assault by racist New York city police goons; The forty-one shots that felled Amadou Dialo, by racist white police goons; The horrible slaying of Sean Bell, who was fired upon with over fifty shots by the police; Oscar Grant, who was murdered by police goons.

Moreover, we still have staring in our face the disproportionate numbers of Blacks languishing in Amerikkka's gulags. Not to mention the racist powder-cocaine versus crack-cocaine laws, accounting for the influx of Blacks being ushered into the Prison Industrial Complex in droves, versus their white counterparts (with the cocaine plague both rock and powder being the sinister work of the CIA), all shrouded under the inimical pall of the double-edged 13th Amendment.

Kanye West

Can't forget the gross neglect and abandonment of the Black men, women and children in New Dr Leanain the wake of 05's Hurricane Katrina; with the breaking of the levees still believed by many to be the diabolical work of the racist Amerikkkan government - prompting popular rapper Kanye West to verbalize what Black folks knew all along, but the bought & paid-for Black leaders were too afraid to say (publicly) - that: "President Bush Doesn't Like Black People."

In fact, President Bush's (open) hatred of Black and other non-white' people isn't an isolated sentiment (confined only to him). So, it is an asinine gesture or plain 0 I' naivete on the part of the Black community (at large) to, likewise, think that it can have it both ways. For its double-stance is equally negative, with the one position cancelling out the other - thereby becoming locked in the vicious cycle of Betrayal Begetting Betrayal.

What is, however, appalling and disheartening to witness is the once grassroots, community-based organizations succumbing to this co opted modus operendi, which is shackled to a 'political correctness' which ultimately serves the white power agenda. For example, some time ago, while reading a Muhammad Speaks newspaper I came upon an article written by our esteemed elder Sister railing against the 'irresponsibility' &

Shahrazad Ali

'recklessness' of the white owned & operated news media for neglecting to conceal the identities of those who go forth to snitch to the racist police establishment about the violence occurring in the hood. While, understandably, being concerned about the rampant Black-on-Black violence in the community, she treasonously advocates an "anonymous" co-operation with the oppressor's racist police establishment. Also, inset within the article is a photo of Sister Ali, with a picture of Messenger Elijah Muhammad in the background, who himself has warned that: "Those who become stool-pigeons for the Devil (the white man) will be used up and thrown back to their own people in humiliation." An irony indeed, since sister Shahrazad Ali was complaining about the very thing Messenger Elijah Muhammad said they would do. And this irony is further heightened when she spews: *"These are bullies who put out the instruction: STOP SNITCHING ... Regrettably, our gut reaction to tell is overpowered by the fact that we will not be protected by the police - or anyone else - after our admission ... When newspapers, police, television, and radio broadcast agencies recklessly report our names and plaster our faces across every media."* - OCTOBER 2007 - VOL. 7, NO.5 ---

Coming from a sister who once advocated (even propagated) more grassroots, revolutionary views for the overall empowerment of Blacks, it is sad to see her deviate from her original position. I mean, here's a sister who, throughout her many years of teaching, never missed on opportunity to point out the inherent injustice in Amerikkka's JUST-US system, as it ill-effects Blacks. Nonetheless, in the same article she further states; "Public exposure of witnesses undermines the entire justice system." As if any Black stands a chance at getting real justice from the oppressor's JUST-US system; and that Prisons or being held captive by the racist white oppressor is the answer or solution to the violence (and other problems) plaguing the Black colony.

Interestingly though, she's not alone in her capitulation, as it has become common to see the once strong and commanding presence of Black men (in general), but the men of the N.O.I. in particular, become compromised, and gradually matriculated into the mainstream political matrix of inept complacency in many cities across Amerikkka. I mean, it has become commonplace to hear Ministers instructing The Brothers (and Sisters) to cooperate with the oppressor's police establishment. This goes against the very foundation of the movement; and furthermore, squanders its once viable distinction of being one of the most credible and respected formations in the Black community. The same is true of the Black Church and many other "grassroots" organizations. The reality is - to effectively contend with the snitch factor, every other form of betrayal has to be exposed and ultimately uprooted. And this can only be achieved by the conscious-minded women & men of the communities affected by these social defects. It is past time for the antiquated methods that have proven futile (in the big picture) to be put to torch; and more revolutionary, hands-on methods espoused. There's no way around it. This is no time for political posturing. And cowards and 'negroes' need not apply!

The only solution is to return to GROUND ZERO; to take up and re-ignite the revolution; with a strong Black Nationalist agenda being the core catalyst. Because without the resurrection of the cultural -consciousness of the Black colony being the guiding force, all other efforts will amount to an exercise in inverted futility.

Members of a community can only respect their community by first respecting themselves. And they will only respect themselves when they are fully awakened to self-knowledge, thus self-worth. And self-worth is inextricably tied to one's culture. It should already be clear that Eurocentric culture isn't going to cut it. For it is under the inebriating influence of European cultural domination that we experience such Black self-hatred and every other pejorative consequence derived from said foreign culture (in the first place); including the remorseless killing of self and kind, snitching on one's peers, etc.

Sure, I know it has become fashionable to utter: "STOP BLAMING THE WHITE MAN" (as a reverse-psychological ploy) to absolve whites of their historical (and current) culpability for the physical ' (and mental) enslavement of Black people, but this study contends that such an argument can only be applied to Black peoples' refusal to return to their cultural ways & principles (after being awakened), not their removal from them.

"However, we have to deal with people who betray our revolution and we have to identify them and punish them in such a way that others will have second thoughts about betrayal" - JOHN HENRIK CLARK

32

"Can It be an accident that the only people who have built an entire culture based on the dominance of others are also the only ones who are Caucasian?"

--- MARIMBA ANI (YURUGU)

Author Dr. Marimba Ani

Hence, for Blacks to attempt to remedy the calamities of their community, minus their collective cultural repatriation, delineates an inevitable cycle of failure. One cannot "function from both ignorance & intelligence (simultaneously) and expect to achieve ideal results. Likewise, one cannot be both European & Afrikan or problem and solution, and expect positive results. If a real remedy is to be achieved, the community has to make a choice. And if its choice doesn't involve the reclamation of its own cultural ways (and the discarding of European cultural ways) its problems will persist. It is as simple as that. And this will require a bona fide, defacto revolution.

"In a revolution, you do not patch up an old society. You replace an old society. When a society (its ideas & methods) has grown old and weak, fat and flabby and fails to serve its people, the conscious role of those who have suffered from that society is not to prop up that society, but to change that society in such a way that it will never be the same again."

--- MALCOLM X

--- DEATH BEFORE DISHONOR ---

"Each generation must, out of relative obscurity, discover its mission - fulfill it or betray it."

--- FRANTZ FANON ---

Frantz Fanon

The phrase DEATH BEFORE DISHONOR has pretty much lost its intended and pragmatic purpose over the years, and have been relegated to a mere empty, rhetorical maxim. This is due, in large part, to People being allowed to dishonor or betray their respective groups, peers, organizations, street-fraternities (so-called gangs), etc., without being penalized or, quite frankly, put to death. And this DISHONOR mainly underlines, but is not necessarily confined to, snitching.

It is via penalties (meted out accordingly) that HONOR is respected and preserved; especially in cases where one has pledged an oath, with the penalty for its breach being clearly understood beforehand. In certain cultures, death is preferable to dishonor, as an inherent principle of character, which is in line with one's cultural imperatives. In this context, one is inclined to sacrifice his life before he allows his social or ethnic group to be cast in the shadow of ill-repute or dishonor (by his deviation from the tenets which governs the whole group). And, for a social or cultural group to maintain its vitality and distinction, it cannot allow its binding principles to be supplanted by others' cultural impositions. In such cases, resistance should be an integral part of the preservation and protection of the group's cultural polity. And

34

this protection hinges on the enforcement of said principles, by the groups warrior-class; even in the face of others' opposing principles.

The moment a group (especially on the racial/cultural frontier) permits another group to define or filter its principles through the opposing group's (cultural) prism, the subject group's (sub-integrationist) co-operation/capitulation will soon follow. Therefore, as an essential element of resistance, secrecy must be a cardinal rule, and its betrayal a cardinal sin. After all, it seems that everybody's got a Secret-Society of some sort, for the benefit of their groups' respective empowerment and fortitude, except for Blacks. When will we learn?

--- PEER(GROUP)PRESSURE ---

In the general vernacular of this society, the term 'Peer Pressure' is often spoken of with negative connotations. And while this view isn't entirely inaccurate, it is a parallax from which it can also be viewed positively, for the benefit of a given group. All groups, whether ethnic, religious, racial or what have you, employ varying degrees and/or forms of pressure to keep its members in line with the groups' core precepts.

In the cultural sense, it is an unspoken rite, with the members of a group feeling innately obligated or duty-bound to function within the parameters of a set of principles or moorings endemic to that group, in this context, pressure is applied more so in what NOT to do, as opposed to it being the other way around, with regards to one's conduct running counter to the groups' intrinsic norms.

It is a given that all groups view something (especially if it is a detriment to the cohesion, well-being and overall continuity of the group as taboo. And any member(s) found engaging in that which has been predetermined (by collective consensus) to be taboo, is (rightfully) PRESSURED to straighten up (of their own volition). This form of pressure is considered Communal Reinforcement, which is a manifestation of the honor and respect borne from the cultural (or otherwise) principles they have in (collective) common.

However, if they persist in their unbecoming behavior then they certainly should be penalized (accordingly) - especially if their behavior jeopardizes others, or cast aspersions on the honor & reputation of the group (as a whole).

In the communal context, particularly as it pertains to Black (Afrikan) people, they naturally display Brotherhood/Sisterhood = Familyhood, as it is an inherent outgrowth of their cultural DNA. Conversely, whenever you see Black people behaving narcissistically you can be sure it is an adopted behavior, from another's culture. For selfishness or individualism is the enemy of any real communal or healthy social group.

So, being here in Amerikkka (A society shaped and dominated by European culture), it has become common to see Blacks mindlessly absorbed in a selfish, individualistic stupor. And this mindset is made all the more inured by the ubiquitous capitalist-driven precepts that shapes the society and the perceptions of its adherents. In this vein, peer group etiquette, virtues, standards, etc., are compromised for (individual) aggrandizement; a trend that is on full display in today's "Pop Culture"; particularly as it impacts the Black community.

--- GROUND ZERO ---

In contrast to European and other foreign cultures, Afrikan customs or communalism isn't predicated or structured on laws which loom as a threat to keep people in order. The very foundation of traditional (pre-colonialized) Afrikan Societies were broadly based on communitarian principles & practice. The competitiveness (in the wanton antagonistic context) found in European dominated societies simply did not exist in traditional Afrikan Societies. Nothing took priority or precedence over THE PEOPLE; Nothing!

The People did what was in the best interest of The People (as a collective). In this (Amerikkkan) society however! the people are generally bred to undermine their fellow-man as a routine course of social interaction, to gain or maintain, an (individual) position of dominance within the social milieu. behavior jeopardizes others, or cast aspersions on the honor & reputation of the group (as a whole).

In the communal context, particularly as it pertains to Black (Afrikan) people, they naturally display Brotherhood/Sisterhood = Familyhood, as it is an inherent outgrowth of their cultural DNA. Conversely, whenever you see Black people behaving narcissistically you can be sure it is an adopted behavior, from another's culture. For selfishness or individualism is the enemy of any real communal or healthy social group. So, being here in Amerikkka (A society shaped and dominated by European culture), it has become common to see Blacks mindlessly absorbed in a selfish, individualistic stupor. And this mindset is made all the more inured by the ubiquitous capitalist-driven precepts that shapes the society and the perceptions of its adherents. In this vein, peer group etiquette, virtues, standards, etc., are compromised for (individual) aggrandizement; a trend that is on full display in today's "Pop Culture"; particularly as it impacts the Black community.

Although snitchin', in its many facets, permeates the entire social landscape of this Society, it is however widely regarded as a violation of the "Code of The Streets"·, and as such, it is therefore considered a COD E among criminals (in particular). Even so, there's no denying that "The Streets" is actually a reference to "The People" or "The Masses". And within a capitalist-crimogenic society which is structured hierarchically, 'The people' are, by their positioning (at the lowest echelons of the capitalist social stratum), naturally at adds with the plutocratic elite. And since the wealthy white elite openly wields power & influence over the society at large they are therefore able to easily control mass public sentiment, via its corporate owned media conglomerates. In this same vein, they define Right & Wrong (in their self-interest).

They manipulate the views of the masses to sway in, their favor.

They dictate the rules and methods of engagement, in terms of how the masses should behave in the society. So, "Crime" by their own defining, is interchangeable (at their slanted discretion). In this way, they are able to instill guilt in those who dare "violate" their self- serving laws.

Interestingly though, the iniquitous distribution of the wealth among THE FEW at the expense & deprivation of THE MANY isn't seen by the ruling elite as a crime. By contrast, any act by the poor masses to acquire or expropriate the coffers of the rich (by whatever means necessary), is! But who's REALLY the criminal here? Well, the answer depends on who you ask. Certainly, it is a parallax. But since the elite (few) possess the means to superimpose their version over that of the masses, and the power to penalize those they deem "criminal", the poor is usually left holding the bag. It is in this context that the ruling elite can, for example, label an uprising or a rebellion a "riot" or "looting" or what have you; when from The People's standpoint it may simply be an act of "Seizing the Wealth of The Land." The ruling elite are completely impervious to the sufferings of the poor & oppressed, so the ruling elite is constantly striving to convince the poor that their lot in life is of their own short- comings, thereby making them feel "wrong" for targeting the elite or the very system that is buttressed on the nefarious dynamics between the two polarizing extremes of the socio-economic classes that are designed to maintain an unequal status quo.

And, these strivings (by the rich) require the perpetual and systematic conversion of the poor to become compliant, cooperative, etc., which entails that they be willing Informants, Rats, snitches, Finks, Stoolpigeons or what have you, at every level of the social structure. This is part & parcel to them maintaining their power and control over the poor & oppressed.

The belief that one is 'wrong' for going against a system or set of rules and policies that perpetuates one's powerlessness, makes one prone or susceptible to "Doing the Right Thing" (on the power-holders' terms).

Ironically, this is the prevailing notion among the poor & powerless; therefore, the motivating incentive for a ready-made quisling. Anyone who thinks they're in the wrong for expropriating from or rebelling against a system that robs the masses and creates poverty & powerlessness, are, at some level or another, on the side of the system whether it be by coercion, manipulation, force, or sheer ignorance.

Even the phrase "Two Wrongs Don't Make It Right" is mere elitist parlance, introjected into the rationale of the ignorant, the poor & powerless, to misdirect and ultimately arrest their ability to define their own reality. For instance, if a man goes in your pocket and steals your money or any other personal possession, and you (eventually) take it back (by whatever means), you're not committing the (second) wrong. You're actually correcting the first one. That is, unless you allow the (real) crook to convince you that you're wrong, too.

This, in summation, the bane of the socio-political chasm. Of course, the ruling elite, the empire state (Amerikkka) has other names for it, to fit within their 'judicial' lexicon. Nonetheless, it should always be consciously understood that many of the actions by The People that are deemed (by the ruling elite) to be "crimes" are acts of necessity or low-intensity revolution, or both:

"When George Washington and company crossed the Delaware, it was" to raid the British, to take money, supplies and arms, even though he was financed by the French and owned slaves. Joseph Stalin robbed banks when he was fifteen to support revolutionary struggle. The Sabate Brothers in Spain were obliged to empty the tills of banks to resist Franco during the Spanish civil war. When Carlos Marighella In Brazil or the Tupacamarus In Uruguay expropriated from the banks to

finance their struggle. It was clear to the press that they were revolutionaries .... But here in the U.S. the government doesn't acknowledge the collection of revolutionary compulsory tax as the work of revolutionaries ... The state must deny revolution and call revolutionary act and revolutionaries something else - anything else - bandits, terrorists, crooks, criminals etc."

- KUWASI BALAGOON

It is by defining, thus controlling the terms, along with the power to penalize, that the rich & powerful are able to coerce a capitulation to their viewpoint. This is especially so with regards to Blacks following the rules set by whites. In this context, Black people, for the most part, feel it is a crime to even conceive a thought outside the confines of white rule or ideology.

Therefore, from the fear of white folks' power, coupled with a (convenient) ignorance of white folks' (criminal) history of stealing this land from the Natives (So-called Indians) using their patented methods of trickery and murder; and the kidnap, rape, murder and enslavement of their (Afrikan) ancestors, Blacks treasonously align themselves with the Devil-incarnate. This in turn breeds the consummate traitor. The wholehearted snitch. And such obsequious "negroes" find comfort in that they consider themselves "Law Abiding Citizens" (abiding by the laws established by criminals). It is indeed the most peculiar paradox. And this paradox also encompasses street-fraternities (so-called gangs); especially since the "gangster" creed has become the prevailing mindset of today's youth. That is, until the cops enter the equation - then squealing becomes the primary method of

42

negotiating a way out - which means that the gangster posture so readily assumed by today's youth is really a pretemporal facade, lasting no longer than the time it takes for the police to read him (or her) their rights (with the right to REMAIN SILENT getting lost in translation). The irony is that, to be a gangster (by definition) literally means that one is a member of a gang (of other gangsters) as the word 'Gang' signifies a group. And since snitching is essentially a selfish act - the very antithesis of group or fraternal loyalty, it brings into question the very principles governing today's street- fraternities, as well as one's (individual) intentions for joining in the first place. Certainly, no viable group or gang or what have you, has as its core tenets, the option to snitch when confronted by the police or any other agents of the state. So what can be said of its influx (within the Black colony)? Surely it isn't a behavior spawned from thin air. And since it can' be generally agreed upon that it is indeed a social defect, it can likewise be deduced that certain elements of our social environment are responsible for its upsurge.

But what exactly are these elements? Well, for sure these elements involve the social interactions among those of a shared environment It is a given that, within a system/society designed to favor one class of people above (and even at the expense of) others, street-hustling or what is called "crime" is an inevitable by- product. But even then, there's a governing set of principles. And when these principles (among hustlers) are not adhered to, it gives rise to all manner of fake gangsters and other colorful opportunists. And these types come at every level of the game. Nonetheless, they all have one thing (in particular) in common: They all have self-centered motives; and in most cases, at the expense of family & friends, or their follow-man (in general). And this runs the entire spectrum of the social landscape.

In the hood, the very worst things a person could he called is a faggot, a rapist (especially of children) and a snitch ... well at least it used to be that way. Nowadays these taboos are allowed to proliferate;' Which, undoubtedly, contributes to the acceptance and regularity of these damning social defects. Therefore, a definitive system of core cultural principles have to be reestablished in order to curtail these practices.

This naturally raises the questions of: Who is responsible for establishing said principles, and, more importantly, safeguarding and enforcing them? Also, who qualifies? Well, first of all, it is a no- brainer that what goes on in, and affects, the hood should be dealt with and ultimately regulated by the hood. The men (and women) between the ages of 15 & 50 (of most racial or ethnic groups) are considered the Warrior-Class or Vanguard class, with their elders being the governing council. Well, the hood isn't any different. Even the men & women who claim to be "gangsters" or what have you, have an obligation to their hoods or respective enclaves. This entails contributing to the collective economy, the safety of its inhabitants, etc. More important still, that the threat of punishments for the violation of any hood codes be made very real. The racist police establishment should meet the Black-Wall of Silence when it comes to the hood cooperating with them.

Toward this end, it should be made clear that 'He who betrays everything, everything (eventually) betrays him.' This is to say:

History dictates that one can't slime or cross his comrades, friends, associates, etc., and expect loyalty (in return). The infamous gangster (who turned snitch) Nicky Barnes, for example, claims that one of the reasons he flipped was because his so-called friends had betrayed him by making moves on his wife, stealing money from him, among other personal violations. And while there is no excuse for snitching, there is still a lesson to be learned here. In fact, the "reasons" range from so-called friends abandoning friends while in peril, especially in legal woes; or someone snitched (first), and as a pay-back the other turns snitch, etc. (these two wrongs certainly don't add up to a right). Again, there's no justification for squealing, but we'd be remiss to just overlook or dismiss the foul acts that have been known to precipitate it. Remember, disloyalty begets disloyalty (on whatever level it manifests itself). Therefore, every element of disloyalty has to be exposed, razed and ultimately put to torch.

It is significant to note that in a study (conducted in the Black colony and in the prison system) with regards to disloyalty (in general) but more specifically as it relates to the level and rapidity of snitching (in the now times) versus that of (back in the day), it was found that: The level of disloyalty, distrust, disorganization and extreme selfishness among today's youth, is exponentially more widespread and unchecked, thereby spawning this seamless segue into betrayal.

This isn't to imply that the practice of disloyalty didn't occur back in the day; just not as openly and fluently, and certainly not without some form of retribution; nor is this an exercise in finger-pointing for the vain sake of claiming one era as better than the other (for antagonistic purposes). It is more so an approach to correcting the overall defect. Therefore, to evaluate the present, it is important to look in the past (as a gauge), to better prepare for the future.

After all, the snitch virus has infected/affected the Black community (as a whole) - in favor of our open enemy. And make no mistakes - snitching is indeed a virus, in that it needs hosts and therefore victims, to proliferate and sustain itself. In this context, it should be understood that snitching ultimately ensures the prolongation of the repressive government's rulership over the poor & oppressed masses. So the government has a vested interest in proselytizing Black and other non-white peoples (in particular) over to its wide phalanx or network of informants, race-traitors, etc. Snitching, (in the big picture) doesn't benefit the hood one way or the other. It is in this vein that the government often projects potential targets in the (false) light of being informants in order to cast aspersions on their characters in order to arouse distrust and suspicion among their respective peer group(s). Ironically enough, brothers & sisters (from the hood) have taken to using this childish tactic, as it has become common for so-called street thugs to call other street thugs snitches - not only (without proof), but ostensibly out of some sort of (personal) beef or jealousies or what have you - in a lame attempt to tarnish their "street -credibility".

Another selfish (and twisted) but related trend is the acceptance of snitches (by the hood), with the 'excuse' being that: "He (or she) never told on ME." And to engage in these behaviors is to endorse or facilitate one's own eventual downfall. For the dynamics of the hood, theoretically speaking, falls under the "Six-degrees Of Separation" axiom, with all behaviors and events that unfolds in the hood literally being inextricably connected to one another.

It's like, for example, selling crack to someone's mother or sister (in the hood) only to (eventually) have it happen to your mother or sister and what not. Or, to cavort with a known snitch only to (eventually) be snitched on by that particular snitch or some other rat that the hood endorsed or allowed to go un-exposed (and unpunished). In summation, what goes around comes right back around (and quickly when it comes to matters of the hood).

It is in the best interest of the hood (as a whole) to chastise or even exterminate rats (depending on the circumstances). The Black colony cannot attain respect or autonomous power and maintain its distinction while it permits snitches and traitors to roam freely in the hood. The hood has a decision to make; it simply cannot have it both ways!

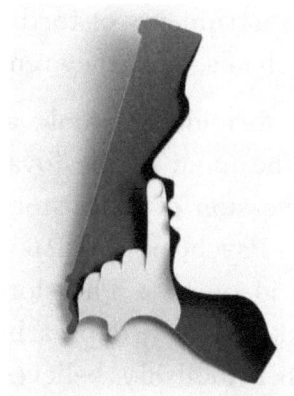

--- BLACK COP ---

TRAITORS, TREACHERY & TREASON

"Just as the slave master of that day used Tom, the house negro, to keep the field-negroes in check, the same 01' slave master today has negroes who are nothing but modern uncle Toms - to keep you and me in check - keep us passive and peaceful. The slave master took Tom and dressed (uniformed) him well, and fed (paid) him well, and gave him a little (mis)education ... gave him a long coat and a top hat and made all the other slaves took up to him. Then used Tom to control them. The same strategy that was used in those days is used today."

--- MALCOLM X

ALTHOUGH SPOKEN in his MESSAGE TO THE GRASSROOTS address over fifty years ago (November 10, 1963), Malcolm's words are strikingly relevant in the now times, as they relate to the modern- day "negro" being employed by his modern-day slave master (the Amerikkkan empire state), to oppress, suppress & repress his own people.

The top hats and long coats have been replaced by the 'uniform', i.e., POLICE, MILITARY, PRISON GUARD, etc. And the infamous whip has been replaced with the baton, stun-gun/taser, pepper spray and other instruments of torture and death. And as for the cuffs, shackles & chains, well, they remain.

Moreover, the most formidable tool at the modern-day oppressors' disposal is the mind of the loyal, modern-day slave. For he is the new-age version of the historical slave. He suffers from Acute Plantation Psychosis (APP). His mind has been baptized in Eurocentric ideologies. Therefore, he sees himself as well as his entire (Black) racial group as inherently Inferior to whites. He sincerely, albeit foolishly, believes that over time, and with "good" behavior and perhaps "higher" education (Further indoctrination), Blacks will eventually be permitted full & equal matriculation into the system of white supremacy.

He even regards the laws & policies legislated and ratified by the oppressor as "OUR" laws & policies. He echoes the deceptive rhetoric: "We're all Amerikkkans" and the like, to justify his open disloyalty to his own people. And since he is devoid of his cultural grounding, he has alternately adopted the views, sentiments and aura of his white oppressor.

Therefore, he seeks the approval & validation of his white master. And is often more brutal and callous toward his own kind than the oppressor himself, to prove to his modern white master that he's REALLY with him. He is the reprised overseer for the revised slaveocracy. He sees the world through European eyes; Hence, he regards his very existence as inextricably tethered to the "'inscrutable" and "insurmountable" culture of white domination. And those who remain on the 'fringes' or 'in the field' - who struggle for freedom (in thought and an autonomous existence) are seen (by him) as radicals, militants, dissidents, even criminal; thus, arousing his (acquired) abhorrence.

And because of this, he is the perfect vessel to be imbued with the aims & purposes of the empire state (its draconian & racist policies, tenets, likes & dislikes, etc.). In summation, he is one of the most treasonous individuals to emerge from the Black colony, in service of the white power structure.

"The black police official or constable of the oppressive state is regarded by his/her oppressed brethren as seven- times worse than the white oppressor himself. For he/she is an outright traitor who dispenses with official impunity, the treachery of the state, against his/her own race."

---IRON EYE

--- THE POLICY CLONE ---

THE TERM "POLICY" is typically defined as a principle or course of action chosen to guide decision making. In this context, and in this society, the decisions that are made are naturally beneficial to those who make them. It is really a matter of power (of the fascist stripe), as opposed to the spurious notion of "democracy" that's rhetorically proffered by the powerful, to give the powerless a (false) sense of 'inclusion' (in the decision-making process).

It is in this way that one is easily persuaded into a "voluntary" protection of the power structure and its constituent policies. Also, while it is generally believed (by the masses) that a policy-enforcer exist for the purpose of 'Serving & Protecting' the public (tax payers), his REAL purpose is to protect the private power brokers (and their interests) - in most cases from the public.

And one would be grossly remiss to overlook the racial factor in this equation, as the very (white) power structure of today is essentially a continuum of its historical model, which is none other than chattel slavery. Sure, the lies and deceptions have been revised and better disguised but the color of power and domination is still white; and the mode of operating is still imperialistic.

And given the history & legacy of the system of slavery and its atrocities against Blacks, which established the current status quo, it is the height of treason for any Black to participate in the protection & enforcement of laws & policies created by whites to protect white power, and to perpetuate their injustices and domination of Black and other non-white peoples. Moreover, the Black man must be completely absent his cultural & moral conscience in order to align himself with his and his people's open enemy. Furthermore, he must be effectively cloned by his European masters. For he is indeed the new millennium UNCLE TOM.

"You're another of the white man's tools sent to spy!"

- Malcolm told Alex Haley when they first met

-- UNITED (POLICE) STATE OF AMERIKKKA --

THE UNITED STATES police establishment is an extension of the slave system. And the Black men & women enlisted in its ranks are the neo-overseers, the black watchdogs for their white masters. They are a part of the (brutal) occupying force in the Black colony; but, conversely, a SERVE & PROTECT apparatus of white society.

They are the DEPUTIZED quasi slave masters, the remote-controlled clones spawned from the womb of white supremacy. And, true to form, they have even adopted their shoot-first-ask-questions- later temperament from their sadistic white masters, when it comes to the way they police the Black colony.

They function within the framework of the pre-projected pall of 'SUSPICION' cast over the hood and perpetually maintained by the many LAW & ORDER type TV programs and the like, the mindless music videos, and the way the white-owned & operated news media frames & contextualizes Blacks versus their white counterparts. Put simply, any Black man or woman (in the Amerikkkan society) who dares to breathe does so within the parameters of being a potential "suspect."

In summery, Blacks are in the "WRONG" for merely existing (in a white dominated society). The Black colony (as a whole) toil in the graveyard of a (collective) character assassination; whereby their systematic annihilation and mass incarceration becomes palatable, therefore justifiable.

Strangely enough, many Blacks (ignorantly) participate in their own destruction by feeding into and perpetuating the very stereotypes that contributes to their (false) portrayal/projection. And since "RACE" is typically concomitant with the brutality that is endemic to an occupying police force, especially as it pertains to Blacks (or other non-whites) being indiscriminately gunned down or otherwise targeted by racist white policy-enforcers (police officers) - the very opposite is argued to explain away the growing trend of black cops murdering young Blacks throughout the Black colony. Take for example, the senseless, unprovoked murder of Sean Bell, who was gunned down by New York city police officers. During the so- called "investigation" the focus was, interestingly, shifted from the fact that he was a young Black man who was unarmed and guilty of nothing more than being (Black) in a white dominated society, to the fact that two of the cops were black (and one Hispanic), downplaying that the other two were white, to dispel the notion of "RACIAL PROFILING" & "DISCRIMINATION". In fact, it was prominently highlighted that, thirty-one of the fifty shots that was fired upon the young brother were "admittedly" fired by one of the (black) cops to reinforce this point. A point that rings moot when one understands that a black cop is merely a clone of his white prototype - which renders him just as - (if not more) dangerous! The hiring of Blacks as cops came full force because of the "Landmark" legislations fought for by the Civil Rights Movement, which espoused a (sub)integrationist doctrine. And so, negro cops get to live out their latent fantasies of being knock-off versions of their white masters. It is also significant to note that, when the modern- day slave master began to notice the wholesale rejection of the "We're all God's children", We're all Amerikkkans" rhetoric, by large segments of the Black community, along with the abandonment of their prior fears and their willingness to fight back against the police, as illustrated by the Nation Of Islam (under Messenger Elijah Muhammad), the Black Liberation Army and other courageous formations, the oppressor came up with the bright idea to employ an "Uncle Tom" class of negroes to police the Black colony. Of course, this fascist pig (in black face)

Honorable Elijah Muhammad

came cloaked in a "race sensitive' pretext. And this line of reasoning, despite its ostensible failure, persists to this very day. It has become obvious that they ultimately serve & protect who pays them; therefore, their loyalties are to the empire state. They have forgotten that we are a nation within (a hostile) nation; that it is betrayal of the first order to join forces with our open enemy, who has a sordid history of kidnapping, raping, enslaving, robbing and murdering our Honorable Ancestors; and now our children. The Black Cop is a TRAITOR!

Coon
Watch

--- BLACK GATE-KEEPERS ---

The Prison Industrial Complex is the new slave ship (on dry land). It is the burgeoning, lucrative new rendition of chattel slavery gone high-tech. Its whitewashed facade and so-called 'legal' trappings attempts to mask the sinister continuity of its historical origins. And just like the police establishment in the so-called 'free' society, it boasts its share of (black) lackey new-age overseers (prison officials). The local, state and federal jails & prisons (plantations) throughout the United States are rife with 'opportunistic' watchdogs, to keep the oppressor's gates and to oppress their own people who, while being a minority in the country, comprise a disproportionate majority demographic of the Amerikkkan prison industry.

In this new slaveocracy arrangement, black 'corrections officers' are often more brutal and hateful than their (white) counterparts/colleagues. They take a special pride in their inflated sense of (make-believe) power over their own kind. However, their own powerlessness within the white controlled Department of Corrections/Bureau of Prisons hierarchy is evident, so they are perpetually vying for the approval of their (white) superiors at the expense of their (captive) peers. The proverbial "pat on the back" from their (white) bosses is relentlessly sought after. Some even contend that they're only employed (in such a treasonous occupation) merely for the paycheck; as if they have an option as to the manner in which they enforce the repressive "Rules & Regulations" established by the white oppressor - or an exemption, for that matter. The job description in & of itself inherently requires a certain type of individual - one who can stomach the man-made hell that was created to subjugate, dehumanize and re-enslave Black and other non-white peoples (even poor whites), not to mention an active participation in it. Strangely enough, black women are increasingly getting in on the act. And, even more ominous, they are often much worse than their male counterparts; mainly because the women, in many instances, harbor a resentment for men; especially Black men. And witnessing the Black man in his powerless state (both in & out of the prison environment) contextualizes and ultimately 'justifies' (in her dense mind) her blatant betrayal. For she openly acquiesces to whom she perceives as the most powerful (in this case, the white man's system).

And in the tradition of Willie Lynch's infamous program (on making the perfect slave), the white man uses the black woman to openly antagonize the Black man (in the prison environment). Moreover, she is the staunchest supporter and advocate for white ideals and all that they entail, not excluding the wretched prison industry wherein she finds a (false) sense of belonging, in league with the oppressor and his power (over her own people); while, ironically, neglecting to recognize the ill-affects of the same power over her own (foolish) self. And, the black cop/guard, both female & male, once used up by the oppressor, will be thrown back to their own people (in humiliation). For they will not, as they so foolishly think, be invited to dine at the table of white supremacy.

The oppressor neither respects nor trusts (black) traitors. He figures if they have no loyalty to their own people then they are less than nothing. So, after their minion duties are thoroughly exhausted they are summarily discarded. SUCKERS!

"If today's prisons are America's new slave plantations, then its black guards are its new uncle toms. And just as the master's second-hand clothes would Imbue the house-negro with a sense of importance and superiority over his captive brethren, the same is achieved with the police/guard uniform; for when worn, it seems to cause the black guard/cop to behave like the slave master himself."

--- IRON EYE

COONBUSTERS
--- UNCLE SAM'S NEGROES ---

EVER SINCE the Civil War era, blacks have been inducted into the white man's Military phalanx. Of course, their (token) 'acceptance' into the ranks of their modern-day slave master's armed forces is made seamless by effectively convincing them that the (illusion) of inclusion into a world of color-blindness, integration and a 'fair' share of the Amerikkkan pie is going to 'eventually' be made REAL.

And since the ingredients in this Amerikkkan pie includes Slavery, Imperialism, thus Global Hegemony, the apt soldier has to be thoroughly bereft of his/her cultural mores, and even more thoroughly indoctrinated and seasoned with the same lust for the destruction of others as his/her master - even against their own people (globally).

For this is the mark of UNCLE SAM'S most loyal 'negro. ' Such a 'negro' becomes like the oppressor's dog, waiting for master to sic him on anyone his master deems an enemy. Just like the historical house-negro, he sees his master's burden (even his wars) as his own. As Malcolm X once pointed out: "If the master's house catches on fire his loyal house-negro says, 'OUR house is on fire'. Or if the master is sick the loyal negro asks, 'massa, WE sick?' ... "

Such is the mentality of the new-wave slave (of today). He doesn't REALLY have a stake in the white power structure, yet he is the frontline defender of it.

This helot-style mentality is displayed by black judges, snitches, black cops; black servicemen (and women), politicians and many others cloned by the co-operative spirit and ideology of Euro-Amerikkkanism.

Colon Powell & Condoleeza Rice

Colon Powell, for instance, is the poster-boy for leading and promoting his white master's capitalist-imperial aggressions against other sovereign nations; mainly Latin American, Middle Eastern and African countries. The latest being Afghanistan and Iraq; with Iran, Syria, North Korea, Somalia and others looming in Amerikkka's hegemonic crosshairs. Condoleezza Rice, who is esteemed with the distinction of being the FIRST black woman to hold the office of Secretary Of (Empire) State, proved to be President Bush's lap-dog, the apt quisling for the white man's rulership over her own people (globally).

And who could forget New York city congressman Charles Rangel's remarks, in response to Venezuelan President Hugo Chavez's statement at the U.N. Security Council, that: "President Bush is the Devil." To which Mr. Rangel later responded: "Nobody talks about MY President that way." Spoken like a true slave! And most alarming is that he spewed this obsequious rhetoric as if it were the views of Blacks (at large). He clearly suffers from Acute Plantation Psychosis (APP); with the irony being that he was recently brought up on charges (by his white master) for "misappropriating" local government funds. FOOL!

And then there's Clarence Thomas, the U.S. Supreme Court justice, or supreme "Token Negro" for Amerikkka's lily-white injustice system. He is another of the white empire's loyal lap-dogs, who has consistently proven to his modern white master that he is a "Good Negro". In a highly (racially) charged case involving Texas Death Row captive Shaka Sankofa (formerly Gary Graham), Clarence Thomas, who was the deciding factor (in a three-judge panel), voted to go forward with the state-sanctioned execution (assassination) of brother Sankofa; even though his appeal was laden with compelling (newly discovered) evidence

pointing toward his innocence; including an eye witness who admitted to being coerced by police, to finger Sankofa (in the initial investigation). Justice Thomas indeed showed his modern master that he is a faithful custodian of his un-just system. Clarence Thomas is a treasonous pariah to the Black Nation! In conclusion, if we (as a Black Nation) expect to become Free Sovereign and respected as such:

Young Shaka Sankofa

"We'd better deal with our traitors. I advocate the reestablishment of the

old Afrikan Blood Brotherhood with an accompanying sisterhood - an internal security force. We won't take you to the white man to be punished, we will punish you so well that we won't have to do it too many times."

--- JOHN HENRIK CLARKE ---

The contents of this little booklet aren't anything 'NEW', nor are they a reinvention of the wheel (so to speak), but an attempt to move beyond empty rhetoric or mere posturing and into definitive action - to become better keepers of the codes that should be held sacred by the hood.

Most groups, whether religious, ethnic, political, secret-society, et al., adhere to certain principles & codes that forbids its members from revealing their respective secrets to outsiders, including agents of the government; in some cases, one agency versus another within the same governmental structure. However, snitching among the denizens of the hood is pretty much 'EXPECTED'. For the hood Is viewed (by all others) as an immoral dumping ground, an insignificant mass of people with no loyalty or binding codes worthy of respect. So, it is time for the courageously conscious to change this perception, as we begin our efforts to organize ourselves into formidable formations to stave off the repressive Amerikkkan government's mission to forge us into agents of our own repression, to do its bidding, in order to ensure its perpetual rulership over us all.

Although the wide-awake warriors among us have warned us for many years that the government possessed far-reaching surveillance capability, we were made to believe that our warrior-scholars were delusional conspiracy theorists" & what not. Well, Edward Snowden's expose of the NSA's universal snooping program should be a wake-up call to us all, of the totalitarian-style police state that's gradually being put in place - with informants and the like, at every level of the social construct, constituting an integral component.

TO THE KEEPERS OF THE CODE

Kevin "Rasheed" Johnson and the stand-up cadres of the New-Afrikan Panther Party; Akode Asafo, Kamau Mwanza Asafo & Mtenginezi of the ASAFO YA UHURU formation; Chairman Knab & General Mandelek of the NATIONAL BLACK LEGATEE ASSOCIATION (NBLA); Mecca Shakur, Etana Shakur & General T.A.C.O.(Wolverine Shakur) of the BLACK RIDERS LIBERATION PARTY; Ministers Alif & Malik Allah and Capt. Jibril of the U.N.O.I.; The stand-Up warriors of the NEW-AFRIKAN PEOPLES' ORGANIZATION (NAPO); The stand-up Gods & Goddesses of the NATION OF GODS & EARTHS; The Akoben House Literati; The Secret Maroon society Combatants; Comrade Tyreek (Puff) the hood General; Brother Capt. Saleem (Kreasy); The "Out Law" J. X Bowie; Brother Khalil (S.T.); General Kareem (K.D.); Queen-Mother Nehanda Asafo; Tahirah Asafo & Iron-Eye (Mchuma-Jicho) of the Pan-Afrikan Blood Sister/Brother-hood; Hakeem 7X (Mwakozi); V. Lombardi (Fidel) of the 46-posse; Queen S.H. (The Secretary); And the many thorough- breads who stand on the principles of 'Death Before Dishonor':

LET THE CIPHER OF SILENCE BE UNBROKEN!!!!

Asafo Chuma Asafo

PRINTED AND PUBLISHED BY:

LEGATEE INK PUBLISHING
1623 Dalton Street #14939
Cincinnati, Ohio 45250
Queen Tahiyrah Asafo Layout & Illustrations
© LEGATTE INK PUBLISHING 2017

www.ingramcontent.com/pod-product-compliance
Lightning Source LLC
Chambersburg PA
CBHW020903310526
45786CB00018B/1652